"DON'T TRUST THE WORLD!!! NOPE, NOT THE CHILDREN OF THE WORLD OR ANY RELIGIOUS ORGANIZATION! WHY? BECAUSE THEY AIN'T GOT A SOUL, BROTHER!"
written by Bill Amor
1st Edition © 2025 by Bill Amor
ISBN: 979-8-9995696-7-7

"DON'T TRUST THE WORLD!!! NOPE, NOT THE CHILDREN OF THE WORLD OR ANY RELIGIOUS ORGANIZATION! WHY? BECAUSE THEY AIN'T GOT A SOUL, BROTHER!"

by Bill Amor

Don't trust the World!!! Nope, Not the Children of the World or any Religious Organization! Why? Because they ain't gotta Soul, Brother!

Summary of Apostle Bill Amor's New Book: "Don't trust the world!!! Nope, Not the Children of the World or any Religious Organization! Why? Because they ain't got a soul, brother!"

Apostle Bill Amor's new book is a bold and provocative exploration of spiritual discernment, inspired by the Amplified Bible (AMP). The central theme of this work is a call to Christians to remain vigilant and discerning in their faith journey, emphasizing that reliance on worldly systems, organizations, or even religious institutions can lead believers astray. Amor challenges readers to place their trust solely in God and His Word rather than in human constructs or ideologies.

Drawing heavily from passages in the AMP Bible, Amor underscores how Scripture repeatedly warns against conforming to worldly patterns. For instance, Romans 12:2 (AMP) advises believers: "Do not be conformed to this world (this age), [fashioned after and adapted to its external, superficial customs], but be transformed (changed) by the [entire] renewal of your mind…". This verse serves as a foundation for his argument that true transformation comes only through God's guidance and not through societal norms or institutionalized religion.

Amor also critiques what he perceives as the soullessness of certain modern religious organizations and individuals who prioritize external appearances over genuine faith. He references passages like 2 Timothy 3:5 (AMP), which describes those who hold "a form of [outward] godliness (religion), although they have denied its power [for their conduct nullifies their claim of faith]." Through this lens, he urges readers to evaluate whether their spiritual practices are rooted in

3

authentic devotion or merely ritualistic habits.

The book further explores themes such as personal accountability in faith, the dangers of false teachings, and the importance of cultivating an intimate relationship with God. Using Hebrews 11:6 (AMP)—"But without faith it is impossible to please and be satisfactory to Him..."— Amor emphasizes that faith must be active and personal rather than dependent on intermediaries.

In addition to theological insights, Amor incorporates practical advice for navigating a world filled with distractions and deceptions. He encourages readers to rely on prayer, study Scripture deeply (as exemplified by the AMP Bible's detailed amplifications), and seek wisdom directly from God rather than placing blind trust in human leaders or organizations.

Ultimately, Apostle Bill Amor's book serves as both a cautionary tale and an empowering guide for believers striving to live out their faith authentically amidst a complex and often misleading world.

List of 12 Chapters for Apostle Bill Amor's Book: "Don't trust the world!!! Nope, Not the Children of the World or any Religious Organization! Why? Because they ain't got a soul, brother!"

The Power of Discernment: Hearing God's Voice Amidst Noise
A guide to developing spiritual discernment through prayer, meditation on Scripture, and reliance on the Holy Spirit to navigate a deceptive world. Pg. 35

Trusting God Alone: Why Human Leaders Will Fail You
This chapter emphasizes placing ultimate trust in God rather than human leaders or organizations, referencing passages like Psalm 118:8-9 (AMP). Pg. 39

Living by Faith in a Faithless Generation
Drawing from Hebrews 11:6 (AMP), this chapter encourages readers to cultivate an active faith that pleases God despite societal pressures to conform. Pg. 44

Guarding Your Heart Against Worldly Temptations
Proverbs 4:23 (AMP), this chapter provides strategies for protecting one's heart from influences that lead away from God's truth. Pg. 47

Building an Authentic Relationship with God
Focusing on intimacy with God through personal devotion, prayer, and studying His Word without relying solely on external religious practices. Pg. 51

Victory Through Christ Alone: Overcoming the World
The final chapter offers hope and encouragement by highlighting Jesus' victory over the world as described in John 16:33 (AMP). It calls readers to live boldly in their faith with confidence in Christ's ultimate authority. Pg. 56

These chapters are designed to comprehensively address the themes presented in Apostle Bill Amor's book while providing practical guidance rooted in Scripture for readers seeking to strengthen their faith amidst worldly challenges.

Introduction to the Book: "Don't Trust the World!!! Nope, Not the Children of the World or Any Religious Organization! Why? Because They Ain't Got a Soul, Brother!"

In a world filled with noise, confusion, and countless voices clamoring for our attention, it is easy to lose sight of what truly matters. The modern age has brought with it an overwhelming flood of information, ideologies, and institutions that often claim to hold the truth. Yet, as believers in Christ, we are called to test everything against the unchanging Word of God. This book is a clarion call to awaken from spiritual complacency and to recognize the subtle deceptions that can lead us away from God's truth.

The title of this book may sound provocative—and it is meant to be. It challenges us to examine where we place our trust and whether our faith is anchored in God alone or diluted by worldly influences. Drawing inspiration from the Amplified Bible (AMP), this work seeks to illuminate how Scripture warns against trusting in human systems, religious organizations devoid of true spirituality, or even individuals who appear godly but lack genuine faith.

At its core, this book is about discernment—a gift that every believer must cultivate in order to navigate a world rife with spiritual pitfalls. Discernment allows us to distinguish between truth and falsehood, between what comes from God and what originates from human or even demonic sources. As 2 Thessalonians 2:11-12 (AMP) warns: "Because they did not welcome the love of the truth so as to be saved…God sends upon them a misleading influence (a working of error) and a strong delusion…" This sobering passage reminds us that without a love for God's truth, we are vulnerable to deception.

Before diving into the themes and lessons within these pages, let us begin with a prayer—a heartfelt plea for wisdom, discernment, and deliverance from misconceptions. May this prayer set the tone for your journey through this book and beyond.

A Prayer for Wisdom and Discernment

Heavenly Father,

We come before You today with humble hearts, acknowledging our need for Your guidance in all things. In a world filled with distractions and deceptions, we ask for Your divine wisdom to illuminate our path. Lord, grant us discernment so that we may recognize Your voice amidst the clamor of competing messages.

Father God, we confess that there have been times when we have placed our trust in people or institutions rather than in You alone. Forgive us for any misconceptions we have held onto—whether knowingly or unknowingly—that have led us away from Your truth. We ask for deliverance from any false beliefs or teachings that may have taken root in our hearts.

Lord Jesus Christ, protect us from falling prey to the powerful delusions spoken of in Your Word. Help us cling steadfastly to Your promises and remain grounded in Scripture as our ultimate source of truth. Strengthen our faith so that we may not be swayed by worldly influences or empty traditions but instead walk boldly in obedience to You.

Holy Spirit, fill us with Your presence and empower us with clarity of thought as we seek understanding through this book. Open our eyes to see beyond surface appearances and reveal what is truly aligned with Your will. May every word written here draw us closer to You and equip us for lives marked by unwavering faithfulness.

We thank You for being our refuge and strength—a constant help in times of trouble (Psalm 46:1). May this journey deepen our relationship with You and inspire us to live out our calling as children of light in an ever-darkening world.

In Jesus' mighty name,

Amen

This prayer serves as both an invitation and a foundation for what lies ahead in this book. As you read through its chapters, I encourage you to keep seeking God's wisdom through prayerful reflection on His Word. Let His Spirit guide you into all truth (John 16:13), guarding your heart against deception while empowering you to stand firm in your faith.

Chapter 1: The Deception of the World: Understanding Its Influence

The world we live in is a complex and often deceptive place. For believers, navigating its intricacies requires discernment, vigilance, and an unwavering commitment to God's truth. In this chapter, we delve into the concept of worldly deception—how it operates, how it influences individuals and societies, and why Scripture repeatedly warns against trusting in worldly systems and ideologies.

What Is Worldly Deception?

Worldly deception refers to the subtle ways in which societal norms, cultural trends, and human institutions can lead people away from God's truth. It is not always overt or obvious; rather, it often masquerades as wisdom, progress, or even morality. This deception can infiltrate every aspect of life—our values, relationships, ambitions, and even our faith practices.

The Bible provides numerous warnings about the dangers of being misled by the world. One key verse is **1 John 2:15-16 (AMP)**:
"Do not love the world [of sin that opposes God and His precepts], nor the things that are in the world. If anyone loves the world, the love of the Father is not in him. For all that is in the world—the lust and sensual craving of the flesh and the lust and longing of the eyes and the boastful pride of life [pretentious confidence in one's resources or in the stability of earthly things]—these do not come from the Father but are from the world."

This passage highlights three primary avenues through which worldly deception operates:

The Lust of the Flesh – Desires rooted in physical gratification or selfish indulgence.

The Lust of the Eyes – Covetousness or an unhealthy fixation on material possessions.

The Pride of Life – Arrogance stemming from reliance on personal achievements or worldly status.

These elements form a framework for understanding how worldly influences can distort our priorities and pull us away from God.

Biblical Warnings About Trusting Worldly Systems

Throughout Scripture, believers are cautioned against placing their trust in human institutions or ideologies. The prophet Jeremiah delivers a stark warning in **Jeremiah 17:5 (AMP)**:
"Thus says the Lord: 'Cursed is the man who trusts in mankind And makes [weak, faulty human] flesh his strength, And whose mind and heart turn away from the Lord.'"

This verse underscores a fundamental truth: reliance on human strength or wisdom inevitably leads to spiritual failure. Worldly systems —whether political structures, economic models, or cultural movements—are inherently flawed because they are created by imperfect humans. While these systems may offer temporary solutions or benefits, they cannot provide lasting peace or salvation.

Consider also Jesus' words in **John 18:36 (AMP)**:
"My kingdom is not of this world [nor does it have its origin in this world]. If My kingdom were of this world, My servants would be fighting to keep Me from being handed over to the Jews; but as it is, My kingdom is not from here."

Here, Jesus reminds us that His kingdom operates on entirely different principles than those of earthly governments or organizations. As followers of Christ, our allegiance must be to His eternal kingdom rather than transient worldly powers.

How Worldly Deception Infiltrates Believers' Lives

One reason worldly deception is so dangerous is its subtlety. It often enters our lives under seemingly harmless guises—entertainment choices that promote ungodly values; career ambitions that prioritize wealth over service; social movements that distort biblical truths for political gain.

Paul addresses this issue in **Colossians 2:8 (AMP)**:
"See to it that no one takes you captive through philosophy and empty deception [pseudo-intellectual babble], according to human tradition [following mere men's ideas of the material rather than spiritual world], according to the elementary principles of this world…"

This verse serves as both a warning and a call to action. Believers must remain vigilant against philosophies or ideologies that contradict God's Word—even when they appear logical or appealing on a surface level.

Recognizing Truth Amidst Deception

To guard against worldly deception effectively, believers must anchor themselves firmly in Scripture. The Bible serves as our ultimate source of truth—a lens through which we can evaluate all other claims or teachings.

Psalm 119:105 (AMP) beautifully captures this idea:
"Your word is a lamp to my feet And a light to my path."

By Immersing ourselves in God's Word daily—studying its teachings deeply and applying them consistently—we develop spiritual discernment that enables us to recognize falsehoods when they arise.

Additionally:

Prayer plays an essential role in seeking wisdom directly from God.

Fellowship with other believers provides accountability and encouragement.

The Holy Spirit guides us into all truth (John 16:13).

Conclusion

Understanding worldly deception is crucial for living out an authentic Christian faith amidst a fallen world. By recognizing how societal norms conflict with biblical principles—and by committing ourselves wholeheartedly to God's truth—we can resist being led astray by false promises or ideologies.

In subsequent chapters, we will explore practical strategies for overcoming specific forms of deception while deepening our relationship with Christ—the ultimate source of wisdom and strength.

Chapter 2: What Does It Mean to Be "In the World but Not Of It"?

In John 17:14-16 (AMP), Jesus prays to the Father on behalf of His disciples, saying:

"I have given to them Your word [the message You gave Me]; and the world has hated them, because they are not of the world [and do not belong to the world], just as I am not of the world. I do not ask You to take them out of the world, but that You keep them and protect them from the evil one. They are not of the world [worldly, belonging to the world], just as I am not of the world."

This passage is one of the most profound and challenging teachings in Scripture for Christians. It encapsulates a central tension in Christian life: how believers are called to live within a fallen, broken world without being consumed or defined by it. In this chapter, we will explore what it means to be "in the world but not of it," how this principle applies today, and how Christians can navigate this delicate balance.

Understanding Jesus' Words in Context

To fully grasp what Jesus meant in John 17:14-16, we must first consider His context. This prayer occurs during what is often called Jesus' "High Priestly Prayer," where He intercedes for His disciples shortly before His arrest and crucifixion. At this critical moment, Jesus acknowledges that His followers will remain physically present in a hostile world after He departs. However, He emphasizes that their identity and allegiance are no longer tied to worldly systems or values.

The phrase "not of the world" does not imply physical separation from society or withdrawal into isolation. Instead, it speaks to a spiritual distinction—a fundamental difference in values, priorities, and purpose between Christ's followers and those who conform to worldly ways.

The Meaning of "In the World"

Being "in the world" refers simply to our physical presence on Earth. Christians live among other people—working jobs, raising families, participating in communities—and engage with culture daily. This is an unavoidable reality because God has placed us here for a purpose.

Jesus Himself modeled what it means to be "in the world." During His earthly ministry, He interacted with sinners (Luke 15:1-2), attended social gatherings (John 2:1-11), and engaged with political and religious leaders (Matthew 22:15-22). Yet at no point did He compromise His mission or adopt sinful behaviors.

For Christians today, being "in the world" means engaging with society while remaining faithful witnesses for Christ. We are called to participate actively in life—to work diligently (Colossians 3:23), love our neighbors (Mark 12:31), and contribute positively to our communities—while maintaining our distinct identity as followers of Jesus.

The Meaning of "Not Of It"

While Christians live physically within society, their spiritual identity is rooted elsewhere—in God's kingdom. To be "not of it" means rejecting worldly values such as materialism, selfish ambition, pride, and moral relativism that dominate much of human culture.

Paul echoes this idea in Romans 12:2 (AMP): *"Do not be conformed to this world [this age], [fashioned after and adapted to its external, superficial customs], but be transformed [changed] by the [entire] renewal of your mind…"*. This transformation involves aligning our thoughts and actions with God's truth rather than succumbing to societal pressures or trends.

Being "not of it" also requires vigilance against sin and temptation. As Jesus prayed in John 17:15 (AMP), *"I do not ask You to take them out of the world, but that You keep them and protect them from the evil one."* While believers cannot escape exposure to sin entirely while living on Earth, they can rely on God's strength through prayer and Scripture study to resist its influence.

Practical Applications for Today

Living as someone who is "in" but "not of" the world presents unique challenges for modern Christians. Here are some practical ways believers can apply this principle:

1. Maintain a Kingdom Perspective

Recognize that your ultimate citizenship is in heaven (Philippians 3:20). This perspective helps prioritize eternal values over temporary concerns like wealth or status.

Regularly reflect on Scripture passages like Colossians 3:2 (AMP): *"Set your mind and keep focused habitually on things above [the heavenly things], not on things that are on earth [which have only temporal value]."*

17

2. Engage Without Compromise

Participate actively in society—whether through work, politics, education, or entertainment—but draw clear boundaries when cultural practices conflict with biblical principles.

For example:

3. Be Salt and Light

As Jesus taught in Matthew 5:13-16 (AMP), Christians are called both salt—to preserve goodness—and light—to illuminate truth—in a darkened world.

This involves sharing your faith boldly yet respectfully while demonstrating Christlike character through actions such as kindness toward strangers or forgiveness toward enemies.

4. Guard Against Worldly Influences

Evaluate media consumption habits carefully; avoid content promoting ungodly values.

Surround yourself with fellow believers who encourage spiritual growth rather than pulling you toward compromise (Hebrews 10:24-25).

Conclusion

To be "in" but "not of" the world is one of Christianity's greatest paradoxes—and challenges—but also one filled with purpose and hope. By staying rooted firmly in Christ while engaging lovingly yet discerningly with others around us every day according-to-God's-word!

Chapter 3: The Soullessness of Modern Institutions
Examining how some religious organizations and societal structures prioritize appearances, power, and wealth over genuine faith and spiritual growth.

In this chapter, Apostle Bill Amor delves into a critical examination of modern institutions—both religious and secular—that have strayed from their intended purpose of fostering spiritual growth and moral integrity. He argues that many of these organizations have become hollow shells, prioritizing external appearances, power dynamics, and material wealth over the cultivation of genuine faith and a deep relationship with God.

The Illusion of Godliness

Apostle Amor begins by addressing the phenomenon described in 2 Timothy 3:5 (AMP): "Holding to a form of [outward] godliness (religion), although they have denied its power [for their conduct nullifies their claim of faith]." This verse serves as a cornerstone for his critique. He explains that many institutions today present themselves as bastions of morality and spirituality but lack the transformative power that comes from true devotion to God.

Amor highlights how outward displays—such as grandiose buildings, elaborate ceremonies, or charismatic leaders—can mask an absence of genuine spiritual substance. These organizations may appear righteous on the surface but fail to nurture the souls of their followers or lead them toward authentic faith. Instead, they often focus on maintaining their image or expanding their influence.

The Pursuit of Power and Wealth

One of the most troubling trends Amor identifies is the pursuit of power and wealth within both religious organizations and societal structures. He references Matthew 6:24 (AMP), which states: "No one can serve two masters; for either he will hate the one and love the other, or he will stand devotedly by the one and despise the other. You cannot serve God and mammon [money, possessions, fame, status, or whatever is valued more than the Lord]."

Amor argues that when institutions prioritize financial gain or political clout over spiritual well-being, they lose sight of their divine mission. He critiques practices such as excessive fundraising campaigns that exploit congregants' generosity without transparency about how funds are used. Similarly, he condemns alliances between religious groups and political entities that compromise moral principles for worldly influence.

The Danger of Superficial Faith

Another key issue Amor addresses is the promotion of superficial faith within these institutions. He warns against teachings that emphasize prosperity or self-help over repentance, humility, and obedience to God's Word. Citing James 1:22 (AMP)—"But prove yourselves doers of the word [actively and continually obeying God's precepts], and not merely listeners [who hear the word but fail to internalize its meaning], deluding yourselves [by unsound reasoning contrary to the truth],"—he urges believers to seek deeper understanding rather than settling for feel-good messages devoid of biblical truth.

Amor also critiques how some organizations use fear tactics or guilt to manipulate followers into compliance rather than encouraging them to grow in love for God. This approach creates a culture where individuals conform outwardly but lack inner transformation.

A Call for Authenticity

Despite his criticisms, Apostle Amor offers hope by calling for a return to authenticity in both personal faith and institutional practices. He encourages readers to evaluate whether their own beliefs align with Scripture rather than blindly following traditions or charismatic leaders. Additionally, he challenges religious organizations to prioritize discipleship over membership numbers and service over self-promotion.

To illustrate this point further, Amor references Micah 6:8 (AMP): "He has told you, O man, what is good; And what does the Lord require of you Except to be just, and to love [and diligently practice] kindness (compassion), And to walk humbly with your God [setting aside any overblown sense of importance or self-righteousness]?" This verse encapsulates his vision for what institutions should strive toward—a humble commitment to justice, compassion, and genuine worship.

Conclusion

In conclusion, Chapter 3 serves as both a critique and a call to action. Apostle Bill Amor exposes how modern institutions often prioritize appearances, power structures, and materialism at the expense of true spiritual growth. However, he also provides a roadmap for reform by urging individuals and organizations alike to return to biblical principles rooted in humility, authenticity, and unwavering devotion to God.

Apostle Bill Amor

By examining these issues through the lens of Scripture—and particularly through passages amplified in meaning by the AMP Bible—Amor equips readers with tools for discernment while inspiring them to pursue deeper relationships with Christ amidst a world filled with distractions.

Chapter 4: False Teachers and Wolves in Sheep's Clothing

In this chapter, Apostle Bill Amor delves into one of the most pressing issues facing believers today: the rise of false teachers who distort God's Word for personal gain or influence. Drawing from Matthew 7:15 (AMP), which states, "Beware of the false prophets, who come to you dressed as sheep, but inwardly are ravenous wolves," Amor provides a detailed examination of how to identify and guard against these deceptive individuals.

The Warning from Jesus

Jesus' warning in Matthew 7:15 is a timeless message that remains highly relevant in modern times. False teachers often present themselves as trustworthy and pious individuals, appearing outwardly righteous while concealing their true motives. They may use eloquent speech, charismatic personalities, or even acts of kindness to gain followers. However, their ultimate goal is not to glorify God but to serve their own interests—whether it be wealth, power, or influence.

Amor emphasizes that these individuals are not always easy to spot because they blend seamlessly into Christian communities. They may hold positions of authority within churches or religious organizations and appear to be devout leaders. Yet their teachings subtly deviate from Scripture, leading believers away from the truth.

Characteristics of False Teachers

Apostle Bill Amor outlines several key characteristics that can help believers identify false teachers:

Distortion of Scripture: False teachers often twist biblical passages to fit their own agendas. They may take verses out of context or reinterpret them in ways that contradict the overall message of the Bible. For example, they might emphasize prosperity and material blessings while ignoring teachings about humility and self-sacrifice.

Focus on Personal Gain: Many false teachers prioritize their own financial or social advancement over the spiritual well-being of their followers. They may demand excessive donations, sell overpriced "miracle" products, or use manipulative tactics to extract money from vulnerable individuals.

Lack of Accountability: False teachers often operate without oversight or accountability. They may reject correction from other believers or refuse to submit to biblical authority. This lack of transparency allows them to continue spreading harmful doctrines unchecked.

Contradictory Lifestyles: While they preach righteousness and godliness, false teachers frequently lead lives that contradict their own messages. Their actions reveal hypocrisy and a lack of genuine faith.

Division and Confusion: Instead of promoting unity within the body of Christ, false teachers sow discord and confusion among believers. Their teachings create divisions within churches and lead people away from sound doctrine.

The Danger They Pose

The impact of false teachers extends far beyond individual deception; it can weaken entire communities of faith. By spreading distorted versions of God's Word, they undermine trust in Scripture and erode the foundation upon which Christian beliefs are built.

Amor warns that following such individuals can have devastating consequences for one's spiritual life. Believers who place their trust in false teachers risk being led astray from God's truth and falling into sin or despair.

How to Guard Against False Teachers

To protect themselves from wolves in sheep's clothing, Apostle Bill Amor encourages readers to take proactive steps:

Study Scripture Diligently: A thorough understanding of God's Word is essential for recognizing false teachings. Believers should read the Bible regularly, meditate on its truths, and seek guidance from trusted sources like the Amplified Bible (AMP), which provides detailed explanations and context for each verse.

Pray for Discernment: Asking God for wisdom and discernment is crucial when evaluating spiritual leaders or teachings (James 1:5 AMP). Through prayer, believers can develop a deeper sensitivity to the Holy Spirit's guidance.

Test All Teachings Against Scripture: As instructed in 1 John 4:1 (AMP)—"Beloved, do not believe every spirit [speaking through a self-proclaimed prophet]; instead test the spirits to see whether they are from God..."—Christians must critically evaluate all teachings by comparing them with biblical truth.

Seek Accountability: Surrounding oneself with mature Christians who uphold sound doctrine provides an additional layer of protection against deception.

Watch for Fruits: As Jesus said in Matthew 7:16-20 (AMP), "You will [fully] recognize them by their fruits." Observing a teacher's actions over time can reveal whether they genuinely live according to God's principles or merely put on a façade.

Conclusion

In this chapter, Apostle Bill Amor underscores the importance of vigilance in identifying false teachers who distort God's Word for personal gain or influence. By heeding Jesus' warning in Matthew 7:15 (AMP) and applying practical strategies rooted in Scripture, believers can safeguard their faith against deception and remain steadfast in their walk with Christ.

False teachers may appear convincing at first glance, but through careful discernment and reliance on God's truth, Christians can expose these wolves in sheep's clothing and stay firmly grounded in authentic biblical teaching.

Chapter 5: Renewing Your Mind: Breaking Free from Worldly Patterns

Inspired by Romans 12:2 (AMP), Apostle Bill Amor dedicates this chapter to the transformative process of renewing one's mind. The verse, which reads, "Do not be conformed to this world (this age), [fashioned after and adapted to its external, superficial customs], but be transformed (changed) by the [entire] renewal of your mind [by its new ideals and its new attitude], so that you may prove [for yourselves] what the will of God is, that which is good and acceptable and perfect [in His plan and purpose for you]," serves as the foundation for this chapter's message. Amor emphasizes that breaking free from worldly patterns requires intentional effort, spiritual discipline, and reliance on God's Word.

Understanding Worldly Patterns

Amor begins by explaining what he means by "worldly patterns." These are behaviors, ideologies, and practices that align with societal norms rather than biblical principles. He points out how these patterns often prioritize materialism, self-centeredness, and superficial values over spiritual growth and godliness. Drawing from 1 John 2:15-16 (AMP)—"Do not love the world [of sin that opposes God and His precepts], nor the things that are in the world..."—he warns readers about the dangers of becoming entangled in a culture that contradicts God's teachings.

Amor argues that worldly patterns can subtly infiltrate even a believer's life through media consumption, peer pressure, or misguided religious traditions. He challenges readers to critically evaluate their thoughts, actions, and priorities to identify areas where they may have unknowingly conformed to these patterns.

The Process of Renewal

The heart of this chapter lies in practical steps for renewing one's mind. Amor outlines three key disciplines:

1. Immersing Yourself in Scripture

Amor stresses the importance of daily Bible study as a means of aligning one's thoughts with God's truth. He encourages readers to use tools like the Amplified Bible (AMP) for deeper understanding. By meditating on verses such as Philippians 4:8 (AMP)—"Whatever is true... whatever is honorable... whatever is pure... think continually on these things"—believers can replace negative or worldly thoughts with godly ones.

He also suggests memorizing Scripture as a way to internalize God's Word. For example, Psalm 119:11 (AMP) says, "Your word I have treasured and stored in my heart..."

2. Prayer as a Transformative Tool

Prayer is presented as both a weapon against worldly influences and a means of drawing closer to God. Amor advises readers to pray specifically for wisdom and discernment when faced with decisions or temptations.

He highlights James 1:5 (AMP): "If any of you lacks wisdom [to guide him through a decision or circumstance], he is to ask of [our benevolent] God..." Through prayerful dependence on God, believers can gain clarity and strength.

3. Practicing Spiritual Disciplines

Beyond Scripture reading and prayer, Amor advocates for additional disciplines such as fasting, worship, and fellowship with other believers. These practices help cultivate an environment where spiritual growth can flourish.

He references Hebrews 10:24-25 (AMP), which encourages Christians not to forsake meeting together but instead to spur one another toward love and good deeds.

Breaking Free from Conformity

Amor acknowledges that breaking free from conformity is not easy; it requires perseverance and vigilance. He likens it to removing weeds from a garden—if left unchecked, they will choke out healthy growth. Similarly, worldly influences must be actively uprooted through consistent effort.

He provides practical advice for resisting conformity:

Limit exposure to media or environments that promote ungodly values.

Surround yourself with spiritually mature mentors who can provide guidance.

Regularly assess your life against biblical standards rather than cultural trends.

Proving God's Will

The ultimate goal of renewing one's mind is discovering God's will—a life characterized by goodness, acceptance, and perfection according to His plan (Romans 12:2 AMP). Amor concludes the chapter by encouraging readers to trust in this process of transformation. As they renew their minds through Scripture, prayer, and discipline, they will experience greater clarity about their purpose and direction in life.

In his final words for this chapter, Amor reminds readers that transformation is an ongoing journey rather than a one-time event. By committing daily to renewing their minds, believers can break free from worldly patterns and live lives that glorify God.

Chapter 6: Faith Over Rituals: The Danger of Empty Religion

In this chapter, Apostle Bill Amor delves into the critical distinction between genuine faith and hollow religious practices. Using **2 Timothy 3:5 (AMP)** as a foundational scripture—"holding to a form of [outward] godliness (religion), although they have denied its power [for their conduct nullifies their claim of faith]"—Amor critiques the prevalence of outward displays of piety that lack true spiritual power and authenticity. This chapter serves as both a warning and an invitation for believers to examine their own faith lives, ensuring that their relationship with God is rooted in sincerity rather than superficiality.

The Problem with Outward Godliness

Amor begins by addressing the issue of "outward godliness," which he defines as religious behavior or rituals performed for appearances rather than out of genuine devotion to God. He explains that such practices often stem from societal expectations, cultural traditions, or even personal pride. While these actions may look holy on the surface, they fail to reflect the transformative power of a true relationship with Christ.

He draws attention to how Jesus Himself condemned similar behaviors during His ministry. For instance, in Matthew 23:27-28 (AMP), Jesus rebukes the Pharisees, saying: "Woe to you, scribes and Pharisees, hypocrites! For you are like whitewashed tombs which look beautiful on the outside but inside are full of dead men's bones and everything unclean." Amor uses this example to illustrate how religious rituals can become empty when they are disconnected from inner faith and spiritual renewal.

The Denial of Power

The phrase "denied its power" in **2 Timothy 3:5 (AMP)** is central to Amor's argument. He interprets this as a rejection of the Holy Spirit's transformative work in favor of human effort or tradition. According to Amor, when individuals rely solely on rituals or external acts without seeking God's presence and guidance, they effectively deny the very power that makes faith meaningful.

Amor warns that this denial can lead to spiritual stagnation or even hypocrisy. He cites examples from modern religious institutions where adherence to rules and ceremonies often takes precedence over fostering a deep connection with God. These practices may provide a sense of comfort or belonging but ultimately fail to address the deeper spiritual needs of individuals.

Authentic Faith vs. Ritualistic Religion

To counteract the dangers of empty religion, Amor emphasizes the importance of cultivating authentic faith. He argues that true godliness is not about performing certain actions or adhering to specific traditions but about living in alignment with God's will and allowing His Spirit to work within us.

Amor encourages readers to reflect on their own spiritual practices by asking questions such as:

Are my actions motivated by love for God or by a desire for recognition?

Do I prioritize personal prayer and Scripture study over attending church events?

Am I open to being transformed by God's Spirit, even if it means letting go of familiar routines?

By answering these questions honestly, believers can identify areas where they may be relying too heavily on rituals instead of nurturing their relationship with God.

Practical Steps Toward Genuine Faith

In addition to self-reflection, Amor provides practical advice for developing authentic faith:

Prioritize Personal Devotion: Spend time daily in prayer and Bible study, seeking God's guidance and wisdom.

Focus on Relationships: Build meaningful connections with other believers who encourage spiritual growth rather than mere conformity.

Embrace Change: Be willing to let go of traditions or habits that no longer serve your spiritual journey.

Seek Accountability: Surround yourself with mentors or peers who can help you stay grounded in your faith.

Amor concludes this chapter by reminding readers that true religion is not about what we do but about who we are in Christ. Quoting James 1:27 (AMP)—"Pure and unblemished religion [as it is expressed] in the sight of our God and Father is this: to visit and look after the fatherless and widows in their distress, and to keep oneself uncontaminated by [the secular world]"—he underscores that genuine faith manifests itself through love, compassion, and integrity.

Final Thoughts

Faith over rituals is not just a theological concept; it is a call to action for every believer. By rejecting empty religion and embracing authentic spirituality, we allow God's power to transform our lives from within. As Amor writes: "True godliness is not found in what we do for others to see but in what we allow God to do within us."

Chapter 7: The Power of Discernment: Hearing God's Voice Amidst Noise

In a world overflowing with distractions, misinformation, and spiritual counterfeits, the ability to discern God's voice is not just a luxury—it is a necessity. Apostle Bill Amor dedicates this chapter to equipping believers with the tools they need to develop spiritual discernment. He emphasizes that discernment is not an innate skill but a gift from God that must be cultivated through intentional practices such as prayer in secret, meditation on Scripture, and reliance on the Holy Spirit.

The Importance of Discernment

Discernment is the ability to distinguish between truth and falsehood, good and evil, and God's will versus human or worldly desires. In 1 John 4:1 (AMP), believers are instructed: "Beloved, do not believe every spirit [speaking through a self-proclaimed prophet]; instead test the spirits to see whether they are from God...". This verse highlights the importance of testing what we hear and experience against the truth of God's Word. Without discernment, Christians risk being led astray by deceptive teachings or worldly influences.

Amor begins this chapter by addressing the dangers of spiritual complacency. He warns that failing to seek discernment can leave believers vulnerable to manipulation by false prophets, secular ideologies, or even their own misguided emotions. He writes: "The enemy thrives in confusion and noise. If you cannot hear God clearly amidst the chaos, you will inevitably follow voices that lead you away from Him."

Prayer in Secret: A Gateway to Clarity

One of the foundational practices for developing discernment is prayer —specifically prayer conducted in secret. Jesus Himself modeled this practice in Matthew 6:6 (AMP): "But when you pray, go into your most private room, close the door and pray to your Father who is in secret…". Amor explains that praying in solitude allows believers to shut out external distractions and focus entirely on communing with God.

Amor encourages readers to establish a consistent routine of private prayer. He suggests setting aside specific times each day for uninterrupted conversation with God. During these moments, believers should not only present their requests but also listen attentively for His guidance. Amor writes: "Prayer is not a monologue; it is a dialogue. If you spend all your time talking without pausing to listen, how will you ever hear His voice?"

Meditation on Scripture: Anchoring Yourself in Truth

Another critical component of discernment is meditating on Scripture. Psalm 119:105 (AMP) declares: "Your word is a lamp to my feet and a light to my path". According to Amor, immersing oneself in God's Word provides an unshakable foundation for distinguishing truth from lies.

Amor advises readers to approach Scripture with both reverence and curiosity. Rather than skimming through passages or relying solely on sermons for understanding, he encourages deep study and reflection. He writes: "The Bible is not just a book; it is the living Word of God. Every verse contains wisdom waiting to be uncovered if you take the time to meditate on it."

To aid in this process, Amor recommends using tools like concordances or study guides (such as those found alongside Amplified Bible translations) to gain deeper insights into biblical texts. Additionally, he suggests memorizing key verses so that they can serve as immediate reminders during moments of doubt or confusion.

Reliance on the Holy Spirit

While prayer and Scripture study are essential practices for developing discernment, Amor emphasizes that true understanding comes only through reliance on the Holy Spirit. John 16:13 (AMP) states: "But when He, the Spirit of Truth, comes, He will guide you into all truth…". The Holy Spirit acts as both teacher and counselor for believers seeking clarity amidst life's complexities.

Amor explains that cultivating sensitivity to the Holy Spirit requires humility and surrender. Believers must acknowledge their limitations and invite the Spirit to work within them. He writes: "Discernment is not about intellectual prowess; it is about spiritual receptivity. The more you yield yourself to the Holy Spirit's guidance, the clearer His voice becomes."

To foster this relationship with the Holy Spirit, Amor suggests incorporating moments of stillness into daily routines—times when believers can quiet their minds and focus solely on sensing His presence.

Navigating a Deceptive World

The final section of this chapter addresses practical strategies for applying discernment in everyday life. Amor acknowledges that modern society presents countless challenges—from misleading media narratives to peer pressure—but assures readers that they are not alone in navigating these obstacles.

He offers several actionable tips:

Test Everything Against Scripture: Before accepting any teaching or advice as truth, compare it with what God's Word says.

Seek Wise Counsel: Surround yourself with spiritually mature individuals who can provide godly advice.

Trust Your Spiritual Instincts: If something feels off or inconsistent with biblical principles, take time to investigate further rather than acting impulsively.

Pray Without Ceasing: Maintain an ongoing dialogue with God throughout your day so that His guidance remains at the forefront of your decisions.

Amor concludes by reminding readers that discernment is both a privilege and responsibility for every believer. By committing themselves fully to prayerful listening, scriptural meditation, and reliance on the Holy Spirit's leading powerfully equips them against deception while drawing closer toward fulfilling their divine purpose.

Chapter 8: Trusting God Alone: Why Human Leaders Will Fail You

In this chapter, Apostle Bill Amor delves into one of the most critical aspects of Christian faith: the necessity of placing ultimate trust in God rather than human leaders or organizations. Drawing from the Amplified Bible (AMP), he argues that while human leaders may have good intentions, they are fallible and limited in their capacity to guide others perfectly. Only God is wholly trustworthy, unchanging, and capable of providing the wisdom and direction needed for a fulfilling spiritual life.

The Biblical Foundation for Trusting God Alone

Apostle Amor begins by referencing **Psalm 118:8-9 (AMP)**, which states" *It is better to take refuge in the Lord than to trust in man. It is better to take refuge in the Lord than to trust in princes. "*

This passage serves as a cornerstone for his argument. Amor explains that trusting in human beings—whether they are political leaders, religious figures, or even close friends—can lead to disappointment because humans are inherently flawed. Even those with the best intentions can make mistakes or fail to live up to their promises. By contrast, God is perfect, omniscient, and unfailing in His love and guidance.

Amor emphasizes that Scripture consistently warns against placing undue reliance on human authority. He cites **Jeremiah 17:5 (AMP)**:

"Thus says the Lord, 'Cursed is the man who trusts in and relies on mankind, making [weak, faulty human] flesh his strength, and whose

mind and heart turn away from the Lord.'"

This verse highlights the spiritual danger of prioritizing human leadership over divine guidance. According to Amor, when believers place their trust in people rather than God, they risk turning their hearts away from Him and becoming spiritually vulnerable.

The Fallibility of Human Leaders

Apostle Amor provides numerous examples from both Scripture and contemporary life to illustrate why human leaders cannot be fully trusted. He points out that even some of the greatest biblical figures— such as King David and Peter—made significant mistakes despite their deep faith. For instance:

King David, described as a man after God's own heart (1 Samuel 13:14), committed adultery with Bathsheba and orchestrated her husband's death (2 Samuel 11). While David repented sincerely, his actions demonstrate that even godly leaders are susceptible to sin.

Peter, one of Jesus' closest disciples, denied knowing Him three times during His trial (Luke 22:54-62). Despite his eventual redemption and leadership role in the early church, Peter's failure underscores human weakness.

Amor uses these examples to remind readers that no matter how spiritually mature or well-intentioned a leader may appear, they remain imperfect beings who can falter under pressure or temptation.

The Dangers of Blind Trust

40

One of the key messages in this chapter is a warning against blind trust in any individual or organization. Amor critiques what he calls "spiritual complacency," where believers rely entirely on pastors, priests, or religious institutions for their understanding of God's will instead of seeking Him directly through prayer and Scripture study.

He references **Matthew 15:14 (AMP)**:

"Let them alone; they are blind guides [leading blind followers]. If a blind man leads a blind man [both] will fall into a pit."

This verse serves as a cautionary tale about following leaders who lack true spiritual insight. Amor urges readers to evaluate whether those they look up to are genuinely aligned with God's Word or merely promoting their own agendas.

Trusting God as Your Ultimate Refuge

The chapter concludes by encouraging readers to cultivate an intimate relationship with God as their primary source of guidance and security. Amor emphasizes that trusting God does not mean rejecting all forms of human leadership but rather recognizing its limitations and ensuring that one's ultimate allegiance lies with Him.

He draws inspiration from **Proverbs 3:5-6 (AMP)**:

"Trust in and rely confidently on the Lord with all your heart And do not rely on your own insight or understanding. In all your ways know and

acknowledge and recognize Him, And He will make your paths straight [and smooth]."

According to Amor, this passage encapsulates what it means to live a life centered on faith. By surrendering control to God and seeking His wisdom above all else, believers can navigate life's challenges with confidence and peace.

Practical Steps for Trusting God Alone

To help readers apply these principles in their daily lives, Apostle Amor offers several practical suggestions:

Prioritize Prayer: Make time each day to communicate with God honestly about your fears, doubts, and decisions.

Study Scripture: Regularly read and meditate on passages from the Bible (such as those highlighted throughout this book) to deepen your understanding of His character.

Discern Leadership: Evaluate whether those you follow align with biblical teachings; do not hesitate to question or distance yourself from individuals who deviate from God's Word.

Rely on Community: Surround yourself with fellow believers who encourage you to grow closer to God rather than placing undue emphasis on any single leader or institution.

By implementing these practices, readers can develop a stronger foundation for their faith—one rooted firmly in trust in God rather than reliance on fallible humans.

In summary, Chapter 8 serves as both a warning against misplaced trust in human leaders and an invitation to deepen one's relationship with God as the ultimate source of truth and guidance. Through compelling scriptural evidence and practical advice, Apostle Bill Amor challenges readers to reevaluate where they place their trust—and encourages them always to choose God above all else.

Chapter 9: Living by Faith in a Faithless Generation

"But without faith it is impossible to [walk with God and] please Him, for whoever comes [near] to God must [necessarily] believe that God exists and that He rewards those who [earnestly and diligently] seek Him." – Hebrews 11:6 (AMP)

In this chapter, Apostle Bill Amor delves into the profound challenge of living by faith in a world increasingly characterized by skepticism, secularism, and moral relativism. Drawing from Hebrews 11:6 (AMP), he emphasizes the necessity of cultivating an active, vibrant faith that not only pleases God but also serves as a beacon of hope and truth in a generation that often rejects spiritual principles.

The Necessity of Faith

Faith is not merely an abstract concept or passive belief; it is the foundation of a life lived in alignment with God's will. According to Hebrews 11:6, faith is essential for pleasing God. Amor explains that this verse highlights two critical components of faith:

Believing That God Exists
The first step in living by faith is acknowledging the reality of God's existence. In a society where atheism and agnosticism are on the rise, this foundational belief sets believers apart. Amor encourages readers to stand firm in their conviction that God is real, even when faced with ridicule or opposition.

Trusting in God's Rewards
Faith also involves trusting that God rewards those who earnestly seek Him. This reward is not necessarily material wealth or worldly success but rather the spiritual blessings of peace, joy, and eternal

44

life. Amor urges readers to focus on these eternal rewards rather than being swayed by temporary pleasures or societal approval.

Challenges of Living by Faith

Amor acknowledges that living by faith in a faithless generation is fraught with challenges. He identifies several societal pressures that can undermine one's faith:

Conformity to Worldly Values
Modern culture often promotes values that are contrary to biblical teachings, such as materialism, self-indulgence, and moral relativism. Amor warns against conforming to these values and instead calls readers to be "transformed by the renewal of your mind" (Romans 12:2 AMP).

Fear of Rejection
Standing firm in one's faith can lead to social ostracism or criticism. Amor reminds readers that Jesus Himself faced rejection and persecution and encourages them to take heart in knowing they are following His example.

False Teachings
In an age where misinformation abounds, even within religious circles, it is crucial to discern truth from falsehood. Amor advises readers to study Scripture diligently and rely on the Holy Spirit for guidance.

Cultivating Active Faith

To overcome these challenges, Amor outlines practical steps for cultivating an active faith:

Daily Prayer and Communion with God

Prayer is the lifeline of faith. By spending time in prayer each day, believers can strengthen their relationship with God and receive His guidance for navigating life's challenges.

Studying Scripture Deeply
The Amplified Bible (AMP) provides detailed insights into God's Word, making it an invaluable tool for understanding His will. Amor encourages readers to meditate on passages like Hebrews 11:6 regularly.

Surrounding Yourself with Fellow Believers
Community plays a vital role in sustaining faith. By connecting with other believers who share similar values, individuals can find encouragement and accountability.

Living Out Your Faith Through Actions
True faith manifests itself through actions that reflect God's love and truth. Whether it's serving others, sharing the Gospel, or standing up for what is right, living out one's faith demonstrates its authenticity.

A Call to Persevere

Apostle Bill Amor concludes this chapter with a call to perseverance. He reminds readers that while living by faith may be difficult at times, it is ultimately rewarding both in this life and in eternity. Quoting Galatians 6:9 (AMP)—"Let us not grow weary or become discouraged in doing good..."—he urges believers to remain steadfast in their commitment to God despite societal pressures.

Faith may set believers apart from the world around them, but it also connects them deeply with their Creator—a connection worth any cost.

Chapter 10: Guarding Your Heart Against Worldly Temptations

"Watch over your heart with all diligence, for from it flow the springs of life." – Proverbs 4:23 (AMP)

In this chapter, Apostle Bill Amor delves into the profound wisdom found in Proverbs 4:23 (AMP), emphasizing the importance of guarding one's heart as a central tenet of living a faithful and God-centered life. The heart, as described in Scripture, is not merely an organ but represents the core of one's being—encompassing thoughts, emotions, willpower, and spiritual inclinations. Protecting this vital center is essential for maintaining alignment with God's truth and resisting the pull of worldly temptations.

The Heart as the Source of Life

Proverbs 4:23 (AMP) states that "from [the heart] flow the springs of life." This metaphor illustrates how every aspect of a person's life—decisions, actions, relationships, and spiritual health—originates from what resides in their heart. If the heart is filled with godly wisdom and truth, it will produce righteousness and peace. Conversely, if it becomes polluted by worldly influences or sinful desires, it can lead to spiritual decay and separation from God.

Apostle Amor explains that guarding the heart requires vigilance because it is constantly under attack from external forces such as societal pressures, media influences, materialism, and even well-meaning but misguided individuals. These forces can subtly distort one's values and priorities if left unchecked.

Strategies for Guarding Your Heart

To effectively protect one's heart against worldly temptations, Apostle Amor outlines several practical strategies rooted in biblical principles:

Immerse Yourself in God's Word

Regular study and meditation on Scripture are essential for fortifying the heart against deception. Psalm 119:11 (AMP) declares: "Your word I have treasured and stored in my heart, that I may not sin against You." By internalizing God's Word, believers equip themselves with truth that can counteract lies and temptations.

Cultivate Discernment Through Prayer

Prayer is a powerful tool for seeking God's guidance and protection. Philippians 4:6-7 (AMP) encourages believers to present their requests to God through prayer so that His peace will guard their hearts and minds in Christ Jesus. Amor emphasizes that prayer should be both a daily discipline and a reflexive response to challenges.

Avoid Compromising Influences

Apostle Amor warns against exposing oneself to environments or relationships that encourage ungodly behavior or thinking. He references 1 Corinthians 15:33 (AMP): "Do not be deceived: 'Bad company corrupts good morals.'" Believers are urged to evaluate their associations carefully and prioritize connections that nurture their faith.

Focus on What Is Pure and Worthy

Drawing from Philippians 4:8 (AMP), which advises focusing on things that are true, honorable, just, pure, lovely, commendable, excellent, or praiseworthy, Amor suggests redirecting attention away from negative or harmful influences toward uplifting content that aligns with God's character.

Guard Your Mind as Well as Your Heart

The mind plays a crucial role in shaping what enters the heart.

48

Romans 12:2 (AMP) instructs believers to renew their minds so they can discern God's will rather than conforming to worldly patterns. Amor highlights practical ways to achieve this renewal—such as limiting exposure to secular media or engaging in activities that promote spiritual growth.

Rely on the Holy Spirit
Finally, Apostle Amor reminds readers that they cannot guard their hearts through human effort alone; they must rely on the Holy Spirit for strength and guidance. Galatians 5:16 (AMP) promises that walking by the Spirit enables believers to resist sinful desires.

The Consequences of Neglecting Heart Protection

Amor also addresses what happens when individuals fail to guard their hearts diligently. He cites examples from Scripture where neglect led to devastating consequences—for instance:

King Solomon's downfall due to his divided loyalties caused by foreign wives who turned his heart away from God (1 Kings 11:4 AMP).

Judas Iscariot succumbing to greed despite being close to Jesus during His earthly ministry (John 12:6 AMP).

These cautionary tales serve as reminders of how even those who appear spiritually strong can falter if they do not remain vigilant.

Encouragement for Believers

Despite these warnings, Apostle Amor concludes this chapter with encouragement for readers who may feel overwhelmed by worldly temptations or past failures. He reassures them with Ezekiel 36:26-27

(AMP), where God promises to give His people new hearts and put His Spirit within them so they can follow His statutes faithfully.

By trusting in God's transformative power and applying these strategies consistently, believers can safeguard their hearts against corruption while experiencing the abundant life promised by Jesus Christ (John 10:10 AMP).

"Guard your heart above all else," writes Apostle Bill Amor in closing this chapter; "for when you do so with diligence rooted in faithfulness to God's Word—you ensure not only your own spiritual vitality but also your ability to shine as a beacon of light amidst a darkened world."

Chapter 11: Building an Authentic Relationship with God

In this chapter, we delve into the heart of what it means to cultivate a genuine and intimate relationship with God. The foundation of true faith is not built on external religious practices or rituals but on a personal connection with the Creator. This connection requires intentional effort, devotion, and a willingness to seek Him wholeheartedly. As believers, we are called to move beyond superficial displays of religiosity and instead focus on nurturing our spiritual bond with God through prayer, studying His Word, and personal devotion.

The Call to Intimacy

God desires an intimate relationship with each of us. Throughout Scripture, He invites us to draw near to Him and promises that He will draw near to us in return. James 4:8 (AMP) reminds us: "Come close to God [with a contrite heart] and He will come close to you…". This verse highlights the reciprocal nature of our relationship with God—when we take steps toward Him in humility and sincerity, He responds by drawing closer to us.

Intimacy with God is not about following a checklist of religious duties or relying on others to mediate our relationship with Him. Instead, it is about developing a deep, personal connection that transforms every aspect of our lives. This kind of intimacy requires vulnerability, honesty, and a willingness to prioritize time spent in His presence.

Personal Devotion: A Daily Commitment

One of the most effective ways to build an authentic relationship with

God is through daily personal devotion. Setting aside dedicated time each day for worship, reflection, and communion with God allows us to grow closer to Him and align our hearts with His will. Psalm 63:1 (AMP) beautifully captures the longing for God that should characterize our devotion: "O God, You are my God; with deepest longing I will seek You; My soul [my life, my very self] thirsts for You...".

Personal devotion can take many forms—whether it's reading Scripture, journaling prayers, listening to worship music, or simply sitting quietly in His presence. The key is consistency and intentionality. By making time for God each day, we demonstrate our love for Him and create space for Him to speak into our lives.

The Power of Prayer

Prayer is another essential component of building intimacy with God. It is through prayer that we communicate directly with Him—sharing our thoughts, fears, hopes, and desires while also listening for His guidance. Philippians 4:6-7 (AMP) encourages us: "Do not be anxious or worried about anything but in everything [every circumstance and situation] by prayer and petition with thanksgiving continue to make your [specific] requests known to God".

Prayer should be more than just a list of requests; it should be an ongoing conversation that reflects our trust in His sovereignty and love. Whether we pray silently or aloud, alone or in community, what matters most is the sincerity of our hearts.

Studying God's Word

The Bible is God's primary way of revealing Himself to us. By studying His Word regularly and deeply—beyond surface-level readings—we gain insight into His character, promises, and plans for humanity. Hebrews 4:12 (AMP) describes the transformative power of Scripture: "For the word of God is living and active...penetrating as far as the division of soul and spirit..."

To truly know God intimately requires immersing ourselves in His Word —not just reading it but meditating on it, memorizing it when possible, and applying its truths in our daily lives. Tools like study guides or commentaries can help deepen understanding; however, reliance should always be placed on seeking wisdom directly from the Holy Spirit rather than solely depending on external resources.

Moving Beyond External Practices

While corporate worship services or religious traditions can play a role in fostering community among believers or providing structure within faith practices—they should never replace personal engagement with God Himself. Jesus criticized outward displays devoid of inward transformation when He said in Matthew 15:8-9 (AMP): "'This people honor Me with their lips, but their heart is far away from Me...'"

Authentic faith begins internally—with hearts fully surrendered—and manifests externally as evidence rather than performance.

Conclusion

Building an authentic relationship takes time, effort, commitment and above all else, a genuine desire to connect deeply with the creator of the universe.

Heavenly Father,

We come before You with humble hearts, seeking Your presence and Your truth. Lord, we thank You for the gift of Your Word, which is a lamp to our feet and a light to our path. We acknowledge that in the past, we may have believed lies or relied on things of this world—whether people, organizations, or traditions—that led us away from the fullness of Your love and forgiveness. But today, Lord, we turn to You with open hearts and minds, asking for clarity and wisdom as we seek to build an authentic relationship with You.

Father, we thank You for Your unending grace and mercy that covers all our mistakes and missteps. Thank You for forgiving us when we were blind to the truth and for patiently guiding us back into Your arms. We are so grateful that no matter how far we may have strayed or how deeply we may have been deceived, Your love never fails—it is steadfast and eternal.

Lord, help us to go deeper in understanding the vastness of Your love and forgiveness. Teach us to trust in You alone as our source of hope and salvation. Let us not be swayed by the opinions of others or by external practices that lack true spiritual depth but instead draw near to You through personal devotion, prayer, and studying Your Word. May our faith be rooted in intimacy with You rather than in rituals or appearances.

Holy Spirit, guide us as we seek clarity in all areas of our lives. Reveal any lingering falsehoods or misconceptions that hinder our walk with You. Replace them with the truth of who You are—a loving Father who desires a close relationship with His children. Help us to discern what is good and pleasing in Your sight so that we may live lives that honor and glorify You.

Thank You, Lord, for the clarity You provide when we seek it earnestly. Thank You for opening our eyes to see beyond the distractions of this world and into the beauty of a life lived fully surrendered to You. As we continue on this journey of faith, may we grow ever closer to You each day—knowing that it is only through intimacy with You that we find true peace, joy, and purpose.

In Jesus' name,
Amen.

Chapter 12: Victory Through Christ Alone: Overcoming the World

The final chapter of Apostle Bill Amor's book, *"Don't trust the world!!! Nope, Not the Children of the World or any Religious Organization! Why? Because they ain't got a soul, brother!"*, serves as a triumphant conclusion to his call for spiritual discernment and unwavering faith. In this chapter, Amor shifts from warnings and critiques to a message of hope, encouragement, and empowerment for believers. He emphasizes that through Jesus Christ alone, victory over the world is not only possible but assured.

The Foundation of Victory: John 16:33 (AMP)

Apostle Bill Amor begins Chapter 12 by grounding his message in the words of Jesus as recorded in John 16:33 (AMP):
"I have told you these things, so that in Me you may have [perfect] peace. In the world you have tribulation and distress and suffering, but be courageous [be confident, be undaunted, be filled with joy]; I have overcome the world [My conquest is accomplished, My victory abiding]."

This verse encapsulates the essence of Christian hope. Amor explains that while trials and challenges are inevitable in this fallen world, believers can rest assured in Christ's ultimate authority and triumph over all worldly powers. He highlights how Jesus' victory is not temporary or conditional—it is eternal and complete. This truth forms the bedrock upon which Christians can build their lives.

Living Boldly in Faith

Amor calls readers to live boldly in their faith by fully embracing their identity as children of God. He argues that many Christians fail to walk in victory because they allow fear, doubt, or worldly influences to cloud their understanding of who they are in Christ. Drawing from Ephesians 6:10-11 (AMP)—*"In conclusion, be strong in the Lord [draw your strength from Him and be empowered through your union with Him] and in the power of His [boundless] might. Put on the full armor of God [for His precepts are like the splendid armor of a heavily-armed soldier], so that you may be able to [successfully] stand up against all the schemes and strategies and deceits of the devil."*—Amor encourages believers to equip themselves spiritually for life's battles.

He explains that living boldly does not mean being free from struggles but rather facing them with confidence rooted in Christ's promises. By relying on prayer, Scripture study (especially using tools like the Amplified Bible), and fellowship with other believers who share a commitment to authentic faith, Christians can overcome even the most daunting challenges.

Rejecting Worldly Solutions

A recurring theme throughout Amor's book is his critique of worldly systems and solutions. In this final chapter, he reiterates that true victory cannot come from human institutions or philosophies but only through Christ. He references Colossians 2:8 (AMP):
"See to it that no one takes you captive through philosophy and empty deception [pseudo-intellectual babble], according to the tradition[s] [and musings] of mere men...rather than according to Christ."

Amor warns readers against placing their trust in political movements, self-help ideologies, or even religious organizations that prioritize human agendas over biblical truth. Instead, he urges them to remain steadfastly focused on Jesus as their sole source of guidance and strength.

Encouragement for Perseverance

The chapter also addresses those who feel weary or discouraged by life's difficulties. Amor reminds readers that perseverance is an essential aspect of faith. Quoting James 1:12 (AMP)—*"Blessed [happy, spiritually prosperous, favored by God] is the man who is steadfast under trial..."*—he assures them that enduring hardships with faith will ultimately lead to spiritual growth and eternal rewards.

Amor uses personal anecdotes and testimonies from others who have experienced God's transformative power during times of adversity. These stories serve as tangible reminders that no matter how overwhelming circumstances may seem, God's grace is sufficient.

The Call to Action

As Chapter 12 concludes—and with it the entire book—Apostle Bill Amor issues a powerful call to action for his readers:

Trust Fully in Christ: Place your confidence solely in Jesus' finished work on the cross rather than relying on human efforts or institutions.

Live Courageously: Face life's challenges with boldness knowing that Christ has already secured victory.

Stay Rooted in Scripture: Make daily Bible study a priority using resources like the Amplified Bible for deeper understanding.

Encourage Others: Share your faith journey with others to inspire them toward greater trust in God.

Amor ends with a prayer for his readers—a heartfelt plea for God's peace, strength, and wisdom as they navigate life's complexities while holding fast to their faith.

"Victory Through Christ Alone" serves as both an inspiring conclusion to Apostle Bill Amor's book and a rallying cry for Christians everywhere to embrace their identity as victors through Jesus Christ. It leaves readers equipped not only with theological insights but also practical steps for living out their faith boldly amidst a challenging world.

Heavenly Father,
We come before You in the mighty name of Jesus Christ, our Savior and Redeemer. Lord, we acknowledge Your sovereignty over all things and humbly bow before You, recognizing that apart from You, we are nothing. Father, Your Word tells us that our hearts are deceitful above all things and beyond cure (Jeremiah 17:9). We confess that we cannot fully understand the depths of our own hearts without Your divine light shining upon them. But Lord, as born-again believers washed by the blood of Jesus, we ask for Your Spirit to guide us into all truth.

Father, we pray for every reader of this prayer to receive a fresh outpouring of Your humble boldness—the kind of boldness that comes not from pride or self-righteousness but from a deep love for You and a desire to see others set free from the lies of the enemy. Lord, we know that the devil is a liar and the father of lies (John 8:44), constantly seeking to deceive and destroy. But You have given us authority through Jesus Christ to rebuke him and stand firm in faith.

Lord God, just as Jesus boldly confronted hypocrisy and falsehood in Matthew 23, give us the courage to speak truth in love. Let us not shy away from addressing sin or deception when it arises, whether in worldly systems or even within religious circles. Help us to do so with humility, always pointing others back to You as the source of life and salvation. May our words be seasoned with grace yet firm in conviction, reflecting the perfect balance displayed by Jesus Himself.

Father, deepen our understanding of Your love—a love so vast and unsearchable that it compels us to reach out to those who are lost or ensnared by false teachings. As Jude 1:23 says, may we "save others by snatching them out of the fire," doing so with reverence and fear of You alone. Empower us with discernment through Your Holy Spirit so that we may recognize what is true and reject what is false.

Lord Jesus, fill every reader with an unshakable faith rooted in Your Word. Let them walk confidently in their identity as children of God while remaining humble servants who seek only to glorify You. May they never rely on their own strength or wisdom but instead lean entirely on You for guidance in confronting evil wherever it may arise.

Finally, Father, we ask that this boldness be tempered with compassion—so that even as we rebuke lies and deception, our ultimate goal remains reconciliation and restoration through Christ. Let everything we do be motivated by love for You and for others.

We thank You for hearing our prayer today. We trust that You will equip each one who seeks after You with everything they need to stand firm against the schemes of the enemy while walking humbly before their God (Micah 6:8). To You alone be all glory forevermore!

In Jesus' mighty name we pray,
Amen!

Conclusion to Apostle Bill Amor's Book: "Don't trust the world!!! Nope, Not the Children of the World or any Religious Organization! Why? Because they ain't got a soul, brother!"

In conclusion, this book is a clarion call for believers to awaken from spiritual complacency and reclaim their faith in its purest form—rooted solely in God's truth as revealed through His Word. Apostle Bill Amor has laid bare the dangers of placing trust in worldly systems, organizations, or even individuals who may appear righteous outwardly but lack true spiritual substance. The message is clear: only God is worthy of our complete trust, and only through Him can we find eternal security and purpose.

Throughout this journey, we have explored the profound wisdom of Scripture as illuminated by the Amplified Bible (AMP). We have been reminded that the world operates on principles that are often contrary to God's will and that even religious institutions can sometimes fall prey to corruption and superficiality. Yet, amidst these challenges, there is hope—a hope anchored in an unshakable relationship with God.

As believers, we are called to be vigilant and discerning. This means testing every teaching against Scripture, seeking God's guidance through prayer, and refusing to conform to the fleeting patterns of this world. It also means rejecting fear and embracing faith—a faith that empowers us to stand firm in truth even when it feels countercultural or unpopular.

Apostle Bill Amor encourages readers not only to recognize these truths but also to live them out boldly. He reminds us that our ultimate allegiance is not to any earthly authority or institution but to God alone. By doing so, we align ourselves with His eternal kingdom rather than the temporary structures of this world.

The journey of faith is not without its trials, but it is one marked by profound joy and fulfillment when lived authentically. As Hebrews 12:1-2 (AMP) exhorts us: "...let us run with endurance and active persistence the race that is set before us [looking away from all that will distract us and focusing our eyes on Jesus]." This verse encapsulates the heart of Amor's message—fix your eyes on Christ, reject distractions, and persevere in your walk with Him.

In closing, let this book serve as both a warning and an encouragement. Do not place your trust in what is fleeting or false; instead, anchor yourself in the unchanging truth of God's Word. Remember that you are called to be a light in a dark world—a beacon of hope pointing others toward Christ. May you walk forward with renewed conviction, unwavering faith, and a soul firmly rooted in God's love.

"Trust in the Lord with all your heart And lean not on your own understanding; In all your ways acknowledge Him, And He shall direct your paths." (Proverbs 3:5-6 AMP)

May this truth guide you always.

About Apostle Bill Amor

Apostle Bill Amor's life is a testament to the power of faith, perseverance, and divine intervention. Diagnosed with autism as a child and considered high-functioning as an adult, Apostle Amor has faced challenges that would have broken many. Born into a world that often misunderstood him, young Bill struggled with feelings of isolation and inadequacy. Despite these challenges, he displayed remarkable determination. At the age of 12, he achieved a significant milestone by winning a reading competition—an accomplishment that filled him with pride and optimism. However, this joy was short-lived when his mother tearfully shared devastating news from the doctor: he was not expected to live beyond the age of 28 to 32. This revelation shattered his world.

Overwhelmed by fear and hopelessness, Bill sought solace in his best friend John Straw, only to discover that John had been taken away by his brother Andy. Feeling abandoned and consumed by anger, he fled into the woods near his home. It was there, amidst the trees and shadows of doubt, that he cried out to God in desperation. Bill's life changed forever on that fateful day. As he climbed a steep hill toward his neighbor's house, he encountered what can only be described as a divine vision: Jesus Christ Himself appeared before him at the top of the hill near a chain-link fence.

The image was vivid—Jesus stood before him with pockmarks where His beard had been removed and glistening divots on His cheeks and chin. He did not resemble traditional depictions; instead, He appeared timeless yet distinct from modern trends. This miraculous encounter marked the beginning of Apostle Amor's transformation. From a young boy who felt lost and unworthy, he grew into a man devoted to spreading God's message of love and repentance. Through trials and tribulations—including struggles with literacy—he found strength in faith and discovered his purpose as an apostle.

Apostle Amor's mission is clear: to guide others toward spiritual healing by sharing his testimony of divine grace. With humility born from hardship and wisdom gained through faith, he invites readers to embark on their own journeys toward repentance and renewal.